THIS IS WATER

Also by David Foster Wallace

THIS
IS
WATER

Some Thoughts,
Delivered on a Significant Occasion,
about Living a Compassionate Life

DAVID FOSTER WALLACE

Little, Brown and Company
New York Boston London

Little, Brown and Company
Hachette Book Group
1290 Avenue of the Americas, New York, NY 10104
littlebrown.com

First Edition: April 2009

Little, Brown and Company is a division of Hachette
Book Group, Inc. The Little, Brown name and
logo are trademarks of Hachette Book Group, Inc.

The publisher is not responsible for websites (or their
content) that are not owned by the publisher.

Library of Congress Cataloging-in-Publication Data

Wallace, David Foster.
    This is water / David Foster Wallace.—1st ed.
        p. cm.
    Address to the graduating class of Kenyon College in
2005.
    ISBN 978-0-316-06822-2
  1. Education, Humanistic.   2. Conduct of life.
I. Kenyon College.   II. Title.
    LC1011.W25 2009
    370.11'2—dc22   2008051851

21

LSC-C

Design by Marie Mundaca

Printed in the United States of America

David Foster Wallace was invited to speak to the 2005 graduating class of Kenyon College on a subject of his choosing. It was the only such address he ever made.

THIS IS WATER

There are these two young fish swimming along and they happen to meet an older fish swimming the other way, who nods at them and says, "Morning, boys. How's the water?"

And the two young fish swim on for a bit, and then eventually one of them looks over at the other and goes, "What the hell is water?"

This is a standard requirement of US commencement speeches, the deployment of didactic little parable-ish stories.

The story thing turns out to be one of the better, less bullshitty conventions of the genre...but if you're worried that I plan to present myself here as the wise old fish explaining what water is to you younger fish, please don't be.

I am not the wise old fish.

The immediate point of the fish story is merely that the most obvious, ubiquitous, important realities are often the ones that are hardest to see and talk about.

Stated as an English sentence, of course, this is just a banal platitude—but the fact is that, in the day-to-day trenches of adult existence, banal platitudes can have a life-or-death importance.

Or so I wish to suggest to you on this dry and lovely morning.

Of course the main requirement of speeches like this is that I'm supposed to talk about your liberal arts education's meaning, to try to explain why the degree you're about to receive has actual human value instead of just a material payoff.

So let's talk about the single most pervasive cliché in the commencement speech genre, which is that a liberal arts education is not so much about filling you up with knowledge as it is about, quote, "teaching you how to think."

If you're like me as a college student, you've never liked hearing this, and you tend to feel a bit insulted by the claim that you've needed anybody to teach you how to think, since the fact that you even got admitted to a college this good seems like proof that you already know how to think.

But I'm going to posit to you that the liberal arts cliché turns out not to be insulting at all, because the really significant education in thinking that we're supposed to get in a place like this isn't really about the capacity to think, but rather about the choice of what to think about.

If your complete freedom of choice regarding what to think about seems too obvious to waste time talking about, I'd ask you to think about fish and water, and to bracket, for just a few minutes, your skepticism about the value of the totally obvious.

Here's another didactic little story.

There are these two guys sitting together in a bar in the remote Alaskan wilderness.

One of the guys is religious, the other's an atheist, and they're arguing about the existence of God with that special intensity that comes after about the fourth beer.

And the atheist says, "Look, it's not like I don't have actual reasons for not believing in God.

It's not like I haven't ever experimented with the whole God-and-prayer thing.

Just last month, I got caught off away from the camp in that terrible blizzard, and I couldn't see a thing, and I was totally lost, and it was fifty below, and so I did, I tried it: I fell to my knees in the snow and cried out, 'God, if there is a God, I'm lost in this blizzard, and I'm gonna die if you don't help me!'"

And now, in the bar, the religious guy looks at the atheist all puzzled: "Well then, you must believe now," he says. "After all, here you are, alive."

The atheist rolls his eyes like the religious guy is a total simp: "No, man, all that happened was that a couple Eskimos just happened to come wandering by, and they showed me the way back to the camp."

It's easy to run this story through a kind of standard liberal arts analysis: The exact same experience can mean two completely different things to two different people, given those people's two different belief templates and two different ways of constructing meaning from experience.

Because we prize tolerance and diversity of belief, nowhere in our liberal arts analysis do we want to claim that one guy's interpretation is true and the other guy's is false or bad.

Which is fine, except we also never end up talking about just where these individual templates and beliefs come from, meaning, where they come from *inside* the two guys.

As if a person's most basic orientation toward the world and the meaning of his experience were somehow automatically hardwired, like height or shoe size, or absorbed from the culture, like language.

As if how we construct meaning were not actually a matter of personal, intentional choice, of conscious decision.

Plus, there's the matter of arrogance.

The nonreligious guy is so totally, obnoxiously confident in his dismissal of the possibility that the Eskimos had anything to do with his prayer for help.

True, there are plenty of religious people who seem arrogantly certain of their own interpretations, too.

They're probably even more repulsive
than atheists, at least to most of us here,
but the fact is that religious dogmatists'
problem is exactly the same as the story's
atheist's — arrogance, blind certainty,
a closed-mindedness that's like an
imprisonment so complete that the
prisoner doesn't even know he's locked up.

The point here is that I think this is
one part of what the liberal arts mantra
of "teaching me how to think" is really
supposed to mean: to be just a little less
arrogant, to have some "critical awareness"
about myself and my certainties... because
a huge percentage of the stuff that I tend
to be automatically certain of is, it turns
out, totally wrong and deluded.

I have learned this the hard way, as I predict you graduates will, too.

Here's one example of the utter wrongness of something I tend to be automatically sure of.

Everything in my own immediate experience supports my deep belief that I am the absolute center of the universe, the realest, most vivid and important person in existence.

We rarely think about this sort of natural, basic self-centeredness, because it's so socially repulsive, but it's pretty much the same for all of us, deep down.

It is our default setting, hardwired into
our boards at birth.

Think about it: There is no experience
you've had that you were not at the
absolute center of.

The world as you experience it is there in front of you, or behind you, to the left or right of you, on your TV, or your monitor, or whatever.

Other people's thoughts and feelings have to be communicated to you somehow, but your own are so immediate, urgent, *real*.

You get the idea.

But please don't worry that I'm getting
ready to preach to you about compassion
or other-directedness or all the so-called
"virtues."

This is not a matter of virtue—it's a matter of my choosing to do the work of somehow altering or getting free of my natural, hardwired default setting, which is to be deeply and literally self-centered, and to see and interpret everything through this lens of self.

People who *can* adjust their natural default setting this way are often described as being, quote, "well-adjusted," which I suggest to you is not an accidental term.

Given the academic setting here, an obvious question is how much of this work of adjusting our default setting involves actual knowledge or intellect.

The answer, not surprisingly, is that it depends what kind of knowledge we're talking about.

Probably the most dangerous thing about an academic education, at least in my own case, is that it enables my tendency to over-intellectualize stuff, to get lost in abstract thinking instead of simply paying attention to what's going on in front of me.

Instead of paying attention to what's going on *inside* me.

As I'm sure you guys know by now, it is extremely difficult to stay alert and attentive instead of getting hypnotized by the constant monologue inside your head.

What you don't yet know are the stakes of this struggle.

In the twenty years since my own graduation, I have come gradually to understand these stakes, and to see that the liberal arts cliché about "teaching you how to think" was actually shorthand for a very deep and important truth.

"Learning how to think" really means learning how to exercise some control over *how* and *what* you think.

It means being conscious and aware enough to *choose* what you pay attention to and to *choose* how you construct meaning from experience.

Because if you cannot or will not exercise this kind of choice in adult life, you will be totally hosed.

Think of the old cliché about the mind being "an excellent servant but a terrible master."

This, like many clichés, so lame and banal on the surface, actually expresses a great and terrible truth.

It is not the least bit coincidental that adults who commit suicide with firearms nearly always shoot themselves in . . . the *head*.

And the truth is that most of these suicides are actually dead long before they pull the trigger.

And I submit that this is what the real, no-shit value of your liberal arts education is supposed to be about: How to keep from going through your comfortable, prosperous, respectable adult life dead, unconscious, a slave to your head and to your natural default setting of being uniquely, completely, imperially alone, day in and day out.

That may sound like hyperbole, or abstract nonsense.

So let's get concrete.

The plain fact is that you graduating seniors do not yet have any clue what "day in, day out" really means.

There happen to be whole large parts of adult American life that nobody talks about in commencement speeches.

One such part involves boredom, routine, and petty frustration.

The parents and older folks here will know all too well what I'm talking about.

By way of example, let's say it's an average adult day, and you get up in the morning, go to your challenging, white-collar college-graduate job, and you work hard for nine or ten hours, and at the end of the day you're tired, and you're stressed out, and all you want is to go home and have a good supper and maybe unwind for a couple hours and then hit the rack early because you have to get up the next day and do it all again.

But then you remember there's no food at home — you haven't had time to shop this week because of your challenging job — and so now after work you have to get in your car and drive to the supermarket.

It's the end of the workday, and the
traffic's very bad, so getting to the store
takes way longer than it should, and when
you finally get there, the supermarket is
very crowded, because of course it's the
time of day when all the other people with
jobs also try to squeeze in some grocery
shopping, and the store is hideously,
fluorescently lit, and infused with
soul-killing Muzak or corporate pop, and
it's pretty much the last place you want
to be, but you can't just get in and quickly
out.

You have to wander all over the huge, overlit store's crowded aisles to find the stuff you want, and you have to maneuver your junky cart through all these other tired, hurried people with carts, and of course there are also the glacially slow old people and the spacey people and the ADHD kids who all block the aisle, and you have to grit your teeth and try to be polite as you ask them to let you by, and eventually, finally, you get all your supper supplies, except now it turns out there aren't enough checkout lanes open even though it's the end-of-the-day rush, so the checkout line is incredibly long.

Which is stupid and infuriating, but you
can't take your fury out on the frantic
lady working the register, who is
overworked at a job whose daily
tedium and meaninglessness surpass
the imagination of any of us here at a
prestigious college... but anyway, you
finally get to the checkout line's front, and
you pay for your food, and wait to get your
check or card authenticated by a machine,
and you get told to "Have a nice day" in a
voice that is the absolute voice of *death*.

And then you have to take your creepy flimsy plastic bags of groceries in your cart with the one crazy wheel that pulls maddeningly to the left, all the way out through the crowded, bumpy, littery parking lot, and try to load the bags in your car in such a way that everything doesn't fall out of the bags and roll around in the trunk on the way home, and then you have to drive all the way home through slow, heavy, SUV-intensive rush-hour traffic, et cetera, et cetera.

Everyone here has done this, of course—but it hasn't yet been part of you graduates' actual life routine, day after week after month after year.

But it will be, and many more dreary,
annoying, seemingly meaningless routines
besides...

Except that's not the point.

The point is that petty, frustrating crap like this is exactly where the work of choosing comes in.

Because the traffic jams and crowded aisles and long checkout lines give me time to think, and if I don't make a conscious decision about how to think and what to pay attention to, I'm gonna be pissed and miserable every time I have to food-shop, because my natural default setting is that situations like this are really all about *me*, about my hungriness and my fatigue and my desire to just get home, and it's going to seem, for all the world, like everybody else is just *in my way,* and who the fuck are all these people in my way?

And look at how repulsive most of them
are and how stupid and cow-like and dead-
eyed and nonhuman they seem here in
the checkout line, or at how annoying and
rude it is that people are talking loudly
on cell phones in the middle of the line,
and look at how deeply unfair this is: I've
worked really hard all day and I'm starved
and tired and I can't even get home to eat
and unwind because of all these stupid
goddamn *people*.

Or, of course, if I'm in a more socially conscious, liberal arts form of my default setting, I can spend time in the end-of-the-day traffic jam being angry and disgusted at all the huge, stupid, lane-blocking SUVs and Hummers and V-12 pickup trucks burning their wasteful, selfish, forty-gallon tanks of gas, and I can dwell on the fact that the patriotic or religious bumper stickers always seem to be on the biggest, most disgustingly selfish vehicles driven by the ugliest, most inconsiderate and aggressive drivers, who are usually talking on cell phones as they cut people off in order to get just twenty stupid feet ahead in the traffic jam, and

I can think about how our children's children will despise us for wasting all the future's fuel and probably screwing up the climate, and how spoiled and stupid and selfish and disgusting we all are, and how it all just *sucks,* and so on and so forth...

Look, if I choose to think this way, fine, lots of us do — except that thinking this way tends to be so easy and automatic it doesn't *have* to be a choice.

Thinking this way is my natural default setting.

It's the automatic, unconscious way that I experience the boring, frustrating, crowded parts of adult life when I'm operating on the automatic, unconscious belief that I am the center of the world and that my immediate needs and feelings are what should determine the world's priorities.

The thing is that there are obviously different ways to think about these kinds of situations.

In this traffic, all these vehicles stuck and idling in my way: It's not impossible that some of these people in SUVs have been in horrible auto accidents in the past and now find driving so traumatic that their therapist has all but ordered them to get a huge, heavy SUV so they can feel safe enough to drive; or that the Hummer that just cut me off is maybe being driven by a father whose little child is hurt or sick in the seat next to him, and he's trying to rush to the hospital, and he's in a way bigger, more legitimate hurry than I am—it is actually *I* who am in *his* way.

Or I can choose to force myself to consider the likelihood that everyone else in the supermarket's checkout line is probably just as bored and frustrated as I am, and that some of these people actually have much harder, more tedious or painful lives than I do, overall.

And so on.

Again, please don't think that I'm giving you moral advice, or that I'm saying you are "supposed to" think this way, or that anyone expects you to just automatically do it, because it's hard, it takes will and mental effort, and if you're like me, some days you won't be able to do it, or else you just flat-out won't want to.

But most days, if you're aware enough
to give yourself a choice, you can choose
to look differently at this fat, dead-eyed,
over-made-up lady who just screamed at
her kid in the checkout line—maybe she's
not usually like this; maybe she's been up
three straight nights holding the hand of
her husband, who's dying of bone cancer,
or maybe this very lady is the low-wage
clerk at the motor vehicles department
who just yesterday helped your spouse
resolve a nightmarish red-tape problem
through some small act of bureaucratic
kindness.

Of course, none of this is likely, but it's also not impossible — it just depends what you want to consider.

If you're automatically sure that you know what reality is and who and what is really important—if you want to operate on your default setting—then you, like me, probably will not consider possibilities that aren't pointless and annoying.

But if you've really learned how to think,
how to pay attention, then you will know
you have other options.

It will actually be within your power to experience a crowded, hot, slow, consumer-hell-type situation as not only meaningful, but sacred, on fire with the same force that lit the stars— compassion, love, the subsurface unity of all things.

Not that that mystical stuff's necessarily true: The only thing that's capital-T True is that you get to *decide* how you're going to try to see it.

This, I submit, is the freedom of real education, of learning how to be well-adjusted: You get to consciously decide what has meaning and what doesn't.

You get to decide what to worship....

Because here's something else that's true.

In the day-to-day trenches of adult life,
there is actually no such thing as atheism.

There is no such thing as not worshipping.

Everybody worships.

The only choice we get is *what* to worship.

And an outstanding reason for choosing some sort of god or spiritual-type thing to worship — be it J.C. or Allah, be it Yahweh or the Wiccan mother-goddess or the Four Noble Truths or some infrangible set of ethical principles — is that pretty much anything else you worship will eat you alive.

If you worship money and things—if they are where you tap real meaning in life—then you will never have enough.

Never feel you have enough.

It's the truth.

Worship your own body and beauty and sexual allure and you will always feel ugly, and when time and age start showing, you will die a million deaths before they finally plant you.

On one level we all know this stuff already—it's been codified as myths, proverbs, clichés, bromides, epigrams, parables: the skeleton of every great story.

The trick is keeping the truth up front in daily consciousness.

Worship power—you will feel weak and afraid, and you will need ever more power over others to keep the fear at bay.

Worship your intellect, being seen as smart—you will end up feeling stupid, a fraud, always on the verge of being found out.

And so on.

Look, the insidious thing about these forms of worship is not that they're evil or sinful; it is that they are *unconscious*.

They are default settings.

They're the kind of worship you just gradually slip into, day after day, getting more and more selective about what you see and how you measure value without ever being fully aware that that's what you're doing.

And the so-called "real world" will not discourage you from operating on your default settings, because the so-called "real world" of men and money and power hums along quite nicely on the fuel of fear and contempt and frustration and craving and the worship of self.

Our own present culture has harnessed these forces in ways that have yielded extraordinary wealth and comfort and personal freedom.

The freedom all to be lords of our tiny skull-sized kingdoms, alone at the center of all creation.

This kind of freedom has much to recommend it.

But of course there are all different kinds of freedom, and the kind that is most precious you will not hear much talked about in the great outside world of winning and achieving and displaying.

The really important kind of freedom involves attention, and awareness, and discipline, and effort, and being able truly to care about other people and to sacrifice for them, over and over, in myriad petty little unsexy ways, every day.

That is real freedom.

That is being taught how to think.

The alternative is unconsciousness, the default setting, the "rat race"—the constant, gnawing sense of having had and lost some infinite thing.

I know that this stuff probably doesn't sound fun and breezy or grandly inspirational the way a commencement speech's central stuff should sound.

What it is, so far as I can see, is the truth, with a whole lot of rhetorical bullshit pared away.

Obviously, you can think of it whatever you wish.

But please don't dismiss it as some finger-wagging Dr. Laura sermon.

None of this is about morality, or religion, or dogma, or big fancy questions of life after death.

The capital-T Truth is about life *before* death.

It is about making it to thirty, or maybe even fifty, without wanting to shoot yourself in the head.

It is about the real value of a real
education, which has nothing to do with
grades or degrees and everything to do
with simple awareness—awareness of
what is so real and essential, so hidden in
plain sight all around us, that we have to
keep reminding ourselves over and over:

"This is water."

"This is water."

"These Eskimos might be much more than they seem."

It is unimaginably hard to do this—to live consciously, adultly, day in and day out.

Which means yet another cliché is true: Your education really *is* the job of a lifetime, and it commences — now.

I wish you way more than luck.

David Foster Wallace wrote the acclaimed novels *Infinite Jest* and *The Broom of the System* and the story collections *Oblivion*, *Brief Interviews with Hideous Men*, and *Girl with Curious Hair*. His nonfiction includes the essay collections *Consider the Lobster* and *A Supposedly Fun Thing I'll Never Do Again*, and the full-length work *Everything and More*. He died in 2008.